BIRDS
OF PREY

BIRDS
OF PREY

Grange
BOOKS

A QUANTUM BOOK

Published by Grange Books
an imprint of Grange Books Plc
The Grange
Kingsnorth Industrial Estate
Hoo, nr. Rochester
Kent ME3 9ND

ISBN 1-84013-252-X

This book is produced by
Quantum Books Ltd
6 Blundell Street
London N7 9BH

Project Manager: Rebecca Kingsley
Project Editor: Judith Millidge
Design/Editorial: David Manson
Andy McColm, Maggie Manson

The material in this publication previously appeared in
North American Birds of Prey, Garden Bird Facts

QUMSPBP
Set in Futura
Reproduced in Singapore by Eray Scan
Printed in Singapore by Star Standard Industries (Pte) Ltd

Contents

AVIAN PREDATORS

For as long as mankind has had an imagination, birds of prey have had an exalted place in it. And little wonder – who hasn't stood breathless at the sight of a hawk arrowing through the air, as if earth and sky were at its command, or felt the hairs on their neck rise at the midnight hoot of an unseen owl? They are among the most exciting and beautiful creatures in the world – and magnificent avian predators.

Raptor Characteristics

What is a bird of prey? Not simply a bird that kills other animals. Actually a better term to use is 'raptor', which refers to those predatory birds that have evolved very specialised beaks and talons used to catch their food.

AVIAN PREDATORS

The Latin word raptor means 'one who seizes and carries away', a term that immediately calls to mind the archetypal eagles, the most powerful of all the avian predators. Yet the Falconiformes order – one of the largest and most amazing avian groups – includes an unexpected range of form and habit, from swift, bird-catching falcons, amongst the fastest of the birds, to huge, ugly carrion-eating vultures. Although vultures do not kill their own food, their huge, powerful beak allows them to scavenge the carcasses of other predator's victims.

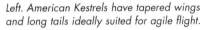

Left. American Kestrels have tapered wings and long tails ideally suited for agile flight.

Above. Swainson's Hawks are typical raptors with a powerful beak and talons.

RAPTOR POWER IMAGE

Raptors' great strength and highly remarkable powers of flight and sight have inspired, enthralled and terrified human beings for thousands of years. So potent is their image, that even today they appear on the crests of many nations including the United States and the flag of Mexico. While their use in military insignia and business logos is widespread, terms such as 'eagle-eyed' have worldwide meaning.

RAPTOR FEATURES

Raptors may show many different forms, but they all share a few common features. The beak is invariably hooked and sharp, to tear food into bite-sized chunks for swallowing. Their feet are strong with sharp curved talons (vultures being the exception). All have excellent eyesight, with eyes in the front of the head affording binocular vision for better depth perception. Most are good fliers, although this trait is not universal.

Raptor Beaks and Feet

Raptors are characterised by hooked beaks, strong feet, sharply curved talons and large eyes. Typically, they hunt by day, and eat live prey caught with their feet. Differences in the basic design are adaptations to the extraordinary variety of raptor behaviour.

BODY AND FLIGHT

The vultures soar on long, broad wings and have strong feet with relatively straight talons; they must search vast distances to locate carrion, then hold it while they tear with their beaks rather than subdue it.

In general, the falcons have a muscular body, long pointed wings and long toes – all features necessary for swift, agile flight and capture of airborne prey. Many of the kites have a slim body and weak fleshy feet which reflect their less predatory habits.

Left. The owl is adapted for night hunting with large eyes and exceptional hearing.

Above. With well-camouflaged chicks, a female osprey delivers a fish to the nest.

EQUIPPED TO HUNT

Some of the large forest eagles have massive legs and powerful talons, and are able to capture monkeys, sloths and other large mammals from the trees. Falcons kill their prey with a blow or by biting their prey's neck in order to severe the spinal cord. Hawks, and other members of the family Accipitridae, kill by the force of their grip, often compulsively squeezing the victim. All raptors use their feet to hold prey and their beaks to dissect it.

RAPTOR PLUMAGE

The plumage of most birds of prey is brown to chestnut, dark grey, or black, with mottled, barred or streaked undersides. A few species are adorned with crests which they can raise in emotion. Some species have a distinctive juvenile plumage and in a few the adult male differs in colour from the female. Females are almost always larger than males especially in an agile bird-catching species such as the Peregrine Falcon.

Territories and Migration

Generally territorial, in suitable habitat, raptor pairs space themselves fairly evenly. For some species, the territory is permanent, but for others it is occupied and defended only during the breeding season. A nest may be built wherever prey is temporarily abundant.

OCCUPIED TERRITORY

If a territory has a good nest site, it may be occupied by successive pairs of raptors for centuries. The Lesser Kestrel typically nests in colonies of about 20 pairs, or even as many as a hundred pairs, perhaps on a cathedral in Europe, an old fortification in Asia or, less often, a well-recessed cliff. The kestrels feed on insect swarms and like other colonial species, hunt, roost and breed together.

COURTSHIP AND PAIRING

Most raptors are ostensibly mono-gamous. A few raptors, such as some harriers are polygamous. The Harris's Hawk is sometimes polyandrous, with several males attending to one female. Almost all raptors have courtship displays, often with mock aerial battles. The male Bald Eagle commonly dives at the female flying below. She rolls, sometimes grasping his feet, and the pair tumble earthwards.

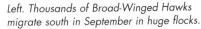

Left. Thousands of Broad-Winged Hawks migrate south in September in huge flocks.

Above. Swainson's Hawk flies south along the Panama isthmus in the great migration.

EGG-LAYING AND INCUBATION

Small species tend to have larger egg clutches and shorter periods of incubation and nestling than large species. A kestrel or falcon may lay four eggs, have a four-week incubation period and the young are in the nest for another five weeks. In contrast, the Black Vulture lays one egg, incubates it for eight weeks and the nestling is in the nest for 17 weeks. A few species lay two eggs but raise only one young – the first-hatched chick kills the second.

RAPTOR MIGRATION

At the end of the breeding season some species migrate. Most prefer to migrate overland, funnelling along land bridges such as the isthmus at Panama on the way from North to South America for the winter: two million birds have been counted, although many more go undetected. They travel as far as 11,000 km (7,000 miles). Other raptors remain in their breeding area year-round, and some are nomadic, wandering wherever prey is available.

Raptor Habitats

Birds of prey can be found in almost any habitat: from Arctic tundra to equatorial rain forest; arid desert to damp marshland; mountainous highlands to prairies and lowlands; farmland to cities.

RAPTOR DISTRIBUTION

Because structural features of the habitat, rather than plant type are most important to raptors, woodlands around the world tend to support a similar range of species. However, raptors are not evenly distributed around the world. More than 100 species breed in the tropics, but only four birds of prey can be found successfully breeding in the high Arctic.

SEASONAL HABITATS

Some habitats support raptors only at certain times of the year. For example, *Buteo lagopus*, the Rough-Legged Buzzard, breeds above the treeline on open Arctic tundra, and then in September, the entire population moves south to winter in farm and marshlands. While Eleonora's Falcon leaves coastal Morocco for the humid winter forests of Madagascar.

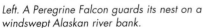

Left. A Peregrine Falcon guards its nest on a windswept Alaskan river bank.

Above. This kestrel is nesting in an old abandoned woodpecker hole.

SPECIALIST RAPTORS

Some raptors can occupy a wide range of habitats as long as there is suitable prey to catch. At the other extreme there are highly specialist species dependent on a particular type of habitat. The Snail Kite, *Rhostrhamus sociabilis,* eats only snails, collecting them in the freshwater lowland marshes of Florida, Cuba, and Mexico, and south to Argentina.

RAPTOR EVOLUTION

Habitat and form can be seen to be linked in the way that each species has evolved. Most forest-dwellers such as goshawks, tend to have short, rounded wings for buoyant flight among the trees. In contrast, open country species have either long pointed wings for rapid flight such as falcons, or long broad wings for effortless soaring such as eagles.

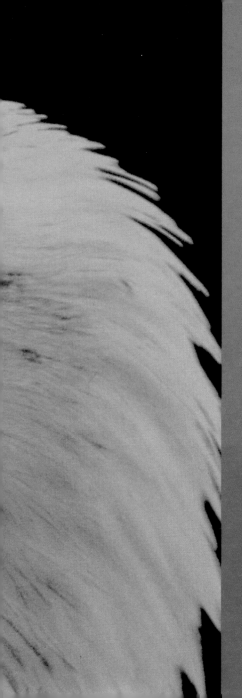

BIRDS OF PREY SPECIES

KEY TO SYMBOLS

A number of icons are used throughout the directory to provide a snapshot of the idiosyncrasies of each species.

HABITAT

Grasslands, moors prairies and tundra			Semi-aquatic and riversides
Woodlands and forests			Mountains and caves
Deserts and arid areas			Buildings and other structures

DIET

Rodents and smaller mammals			Carrion and dead flesh
Fish and amphibians			Snails
Other birds			Lizards and reptiles
Insects			Snakes
			Rabbits and larger mammals

NUMBER OF EGGS

2   Average number in a clutch

BLACK VULTURE CORAGYPS ATRATUS

The smallest of North America's three vultures, the Black Vulture has a very short tail. Nesting in tree cavities or hollow logs, their eggs do not always hatch due to eggshell thinning, which has added to their declining numbers in some areas.

Family Cathartidae.
Plumage All black, with grey head and white wing patches.
Range USA Atlantic coast, south and lower midwest USA states.
Food Carrion.
Nest None built; eggs laid on ground.
Eggs 2; white with brownish scrawls.

TURKEY VULTURE CATHARTES AURA

These vultures use the thermal air to stay aloft for hours, with a few flaps of their large wings. Using sight as well as smell to locate food, they use their hooked beak and sharp talons to tear meat from carrion.

Family Cathartidae.
Plumage Dark brown body, silvery wing linings, naked red head.
Range Southern Canada south to Mexico.
Food Carrion.
Nest None built; cliff ledge, stump or on the ground.
Eggs 2; white with brown spots.

CALIFORNIAN CONDOR GYMNOGYPS CALIFORNIANUS

The largest bird in North America, the Californian condor ruled the skies in the post-glacial days of the Pleistocene. As the climate has changed, and herds of bison, camel and horses disappeared, they became restricted to the Western mountains and coast. Shot for its quills or sport, there were only a handful of condor left by 1980. A captive breeding programme was then introduced to save the remaining birds. The first condors bred in captivity were born in 1989 and the hope is that eventually birds will be released back into the wild.

Family Cathartidae.
Plumage Black body with white underwing patches, orange head on adult.
Range Extinct in the wild; formerly southern California.
Food Carrion.
Nest None; eggs laid on cliff edges and caves in remote areas.
Eggs 1; bluish-white.

OSPREY PANDION HALIAETUS

The osprey hunts by hovering high above water and then plunges, feet first, into the water to catch the fish. Their feathers are oily and almost water repellent. The feet are covered with small spicules that give it a non-slip grip on its slippery prey ; the outer toe is reversible. Its numbers have declined due to eating fish contaminated with toxic chemicals. It is under special protection in Scotland where its numbers are increasing.

Family Accipitradae.
Plumage White below, brown above; dark eyestripe and 'wrist patches' on wings.
Range Cosmopolitan, occurring on every continent.
Food Fish, caught by diving.
Nest Large stick platform built in trees, manmade structures.
Eggs 2–4; white heavily covered with brown markings.

   2-4

Always associated with water, the Osprey, *Pandion haliaetus,* sometimes also known as the 'fish hawk', lives almost exclusively on fish.

AMERICAN SWALLOW-TAILED KITE ELANOIDES FORFICATUS

This is an elegant bird with a white body and black wings and deeply forked tail. Its numbers are declining as the forested swamps and marshlands used for nesting, are destroyed. Pesticides and shooting have also reduced their numbers.

Family Accipitradae.
Plumage White body; black wings and long, forked tail.
Range Southeast USA; declining.
Food Insects, small animals.
Nest Sticks and twigs, built in very high trees.
Eggs 2; white with brown markings.

BLACK-SHOULDERED KITE ELANUS CAERULEUS

Environmental changes have not affected these kites in the same way as other species, and their numbers have risen following their near elimination in Texas. They are attractive birds and are readily identifiable at a distance, by their hunting behaviour of hovering.

Family Accipitradae.
Plumage Adult; white undersides, grey body.
Range Texas, California, Eurasia, Spain, Portugal, Africa, Indonesia.
Food Small mammals, insects.
Nest Large twig cup built in treetops.
Eggs 4–5; white with brown markings.

SNAIL KITE ROSTRHAMUS SOCIABILIS

This is the most specialised of all North American raptors, eating only snails of the genus *Pomacea,* the apple snail which live in flooded marsh grass in Florida. Kite numbers were reduced to about 20 birds but they are recovering in number now they have protection.

Family Accipitradae.
Plumage Male: dark grey, white tail. Female: dark brown, white tail.
Range Endangered; Florida, USA.
Food Apple snails.
Nest Stick and weed platform in shrubs.
Eggs 3–4; white with brown markings.

   3-4

MISSISSIPPI KITE ICTINIA MISSISSIPPIENSIS

The numbers of these birds have increased due to the planting of thousands of wooded shelter belts across the southern plains. In the air, they resemble the peregrine falcon with their long, tapered wings and tail. They like to nest in small towns, and especially golf courses.

Family Accipitradae.
Plumage Adult: grey below, dark grey above with black primaries.
Range Southeast USA.
Food Insects, some small animals.
Nest Stick and twig platform in tall trees.
Eggs 1–3; white.

    1-3

BALD EAGLE HALIAEETUS LEUCOCEPHALUS

Renowned worldwide for it powerful image, this species is still endangered, although their numbers are increasing. Pesticides and illegal shooting had reduced the number of birds and badly affected the laying of fertile eggs. Today, the birds compete at watery recreation areas for food and there is concern that human disturbance may send the number of birds on a downward trend again.

Family Accipitradae.
Plumage Adult: white head and tail, dark body.
Range Breeds coastally, Canada, the Great Lakes, Western USA.
Food Fish, carrion, birds, mammals.
Nest Large, bulky mass of sticks high in a tree.
Eggs 2; white.

An immature Bald Eagle, *Haliaeetus leucocephalus*, which has still to acquire its magnificent adult plumage.

HEN HARRIER CIRCUS CYANEUS

Also known as the Marsh Hawk in North America, this bird spends much of its time near or on the ground in wetlands and grassy habitats. Their breeding is heavily dependent on the main food supply, meadow voles, being plentiful. Harriers do not always mate for life, but where they do their chicks have a better life expectancy than those where the female is left to fend for the chicks herself.

Family Accipitradae.
Plumage Male: light below, grey above with black wingtips. Female and juvenile: brown or rusty.
Range Britain, Ireland, Spain, Scandinavia, widely in N. America.
Food Small mammals, some birds, reptiles, amphibians.
Nest Platform of sticks on a hummock in marshy ground.
Eggs 4–6; white with brown markings.

 4-6

SHARP-SHINNED HAWK ACCIPITER STRIATUS

Although a small hawk, this species does not hesitate to tackle prey much bigger than itself. Song-birds are their usual diet, but pigeons, rabbits and even chickens can be consumed. The female can be half as heavy again as the male.

Family Accipitradae.
Plumage Adult: blue-grey upper-parts, rusty-barred breast.
Range Breeds Appalachians, New England, West USA and Canada.
Food Small birds, some mammals.
Nest Stick platform, usually in conifer in mixed woodlands.
Eggs 3–4; white with brown markings.

   3-4

COOPER'S HAWK ACCIPITER COOPERII

A larger version of the sharp-shinned hawk, this hawk is far less common. There is concern that it may be declining even further. The platform of sticks is usually built by the female but both parents hunt for food for the chicks, although rarely in the vicinity of the nest. Deciduous woods are the preferred habitat for these hawks.

Family Accipitradae.

Plumage Adult: blue-grey upper-parts, rusty-barred breast.

Range Uncommon in USA and Canada.

Food Primarily birds, small mammals.

Nest Large stick platform, lined with chips of bark.

Eggs 4–5; off-white.

   4-5

GOSHAWK ACCIPITER GENTILIS

A beautiful bird, the goshawk is the biggest and rarest of the accipiters. Larger than a crow, they are fast and skilful hunters with a thick body and wide tail. The wingbeats are slow, deep and powerful. Not tolerant of human intrusion, this is a wilderness bird.

Family Accipitradae.
Plumage Adult: grey above, pale grey below, white eyestripe.
Range Morocco, Iberia, Eurasia, Britain, Scandinavia, N America.
Food Large birds, hares, squirrels, crows.
Nest Large, flat stick structure, lined with chips of bark, built high in a tree.
Eggs 2–4; unmarked, off-white.

    2-4

COMMON BLACK-HAWK BUTEOGALLUS ANTHRACINUS

These birds are largely tropical in their distribution, preferring habitats of woodlands and thickets growing along rivers or streams. In flight, it is easy to mistake a black-hawk for a black vulture, although the banded tail helps distinguish them.

Family Accipitradae.
Plumage Adult: black overall, white tail band and white patches under the wings.
Range Arizona, New Mexico, Texas.
Food Crayfish, frogs, snakes, lizards, fish.
Nest Stick structure, lined with green leaves, in tree near water.
Eggs 1–2; white with fine brown spotting.

HARRIS' HAWK PARABUTEO UNICINCTUS

This hawk hunts in a cooperative manner, hunting with up to six birds, which allows them to capture fast running rabbits. They also share the catch.

Family Accipitradae.
Plumage Adult: chocolate-brown body with chestnut wing linings, shoulder patches and thighs; white tail with wide black band.
Range Texas, New Mexico, Arizona.
Food Rabbits, jackrabbits, birds, reptiles.
Nest Stick platform in low tree, lined with green leaves.
Eggs 2–3; white.

GREY HAWK BUTEO NITIDUS

This is a buteo that is flashy and quick, using rapid wingbeats and short glides to snatch prey as it scurries for cover. In size and shape, the grey hawk is quite similar to the broad-winged hawk.

Family Accipitradae.
Plumage Adult: grey upperparts, fine grey barring on the breast, banded tail.
Range Mexican border.
Food Lizards, snakes, small birds and mammals.
Nest Small twig bowl concealed in high treetop.
Eggs 2–3; white.

 2-3

BROAD-WINGED HAWK BUTEO PLATYPTERUS

These birds live in woodland where the trees grow tall enough to close off the canopy and shade the ground. This is a small but chunky raptor, with wide and pointed wings and small head. They regularly fly in large flocks (kettles).

Family Accipitradae.
Plumage Adult: brown upperparts, chestnut-barred breast, wide black and white tail bands.
Range Eastern USA, Southern Canada.
Food Reptiles, amphibians, small mammals, insects.
Nest Small stick bowl, low in trees.
Eggs 2–3; white with buff markings.

 2-3

RED-SHOULDERED HAWK BUTEO LINEATUS

This species, in flight, can be mistaken for an accipiter with its longish wings and tail, combined with rapid wingbeats. These are birds of stream and river valleys, forested swamps and damp woods and are not commonly seen due to the dense cover they frequent.

Family Accipitradae.
Plumage Adult: chestnut breast, black barring on wings.
Range Eastern USA.
Food Small mammals, reptiles, crayfish, amphibians, some birds.
Nest Bulky stick nest, lined with leaves.
Eggs 2–3; pale with brown flecks.

     2-3

SHORT-TAILED HAWK BUTEO BRACHYURUS

A tropical bird whose northern limit is in Florida. This species has colour phases, a light and a dark phase, which are unrelated to age or sex. They hunt by waiting in the wind high above the ground before swooping down quickly to catch the prey.

Family Accipitradae.
Plumage Light phase: white under-parts, brown upperparts. Dark phase: all brown body.
Range Florida, USA
Food Primarily birds.
Nest Twig and leaf in treetop near water.
Eggs 2–3; white often with brown flecks.

  2-3

SWAINSON'S HAWK BUTEO SWAINSONI

This is a big, tame bird, easy to approach, less powerful than a red-tailed hawk. Their feet are small and well-suited to their diet of grasshoppers, crickets and mice. There are two colour phases, the light being by far the most common.

Family Accipitradae.
Plumage Light phase: white belly, brown head and chest. Dark phase: dark brown body and wings.
Range Western Plains of USA.
Food Small mammals and insects.
Nest Large assembly of sticks and weeds, built near the ground.
Eggs 2–3; white often brown flecks.

    2-3

WHITE-TAILED HAWK BUTEO ALBICAUDATUS

One of the largest North American buteos, the white-tailed hawk hunts while soaring and dives quickly to catch the prey. They have learnt to follow grass fires, gathering near the advancing edge of the blaze to catch panicking animals.

Family Accipitradae.
Plumage Adult: grey upperparts, white breast with fine barring.
Range Southern Texas, USA.
Food Small mammals, reptiles, insects, amphibians.
Nest Large, flat platform built in a low shrub with good all-round visibility.
Eggs 2–3; whitish with brown flecks.

     2-3

ZONE-TAILED HAWK BUTEO ALBONOTATUS

This is one of the best birds at mimicry in North America. It is able to mimic the black vulture with its body colour and flight behaviour, and is known to fly with groups, diving when a snake or mouse is spotted.

Family Accipitradae.
Plumage Black overall, with white-banded tail and wing feathers.
Range Texas, New Mexico, Arizona.
Food Snakes, lizards, small mammals, frogs.
Nest Deep stick nest, built high in tree along water.
Eggs 2; whitish with brown flecks.

RED-TAILED HAWK BUTEO JAMAICENSIS

The most wide-spread hawk in North America. This is a robust buteo, adapted to taking a wide variety of prey. Their size depends on sex and geographical region and their plumage is varied with seven colour phases.

Family Accipitradae.
Plumage Highly variable. Adult light phase; brown upperparts, white breast with dark belly band.
Range Northern USA.
Food Small mammals, reptiles, birds, amphibians, insects.
Nest Large, flat stick nest, high in a tree.
Eggs 2–4; white with brown flecks.

FERRUGINOUS HAWK BUTEO REGALIS

The biggest and most powerful of the buteos, these can be striking birds in either light or dark colour phase. They hunt with the same rush and vitality that a golden eagle displays. A mammal hunter, a pair's colony will usually include a large ground squirrel colony.

Family Accipitradae.
Plumage Rusty upperparts, white underparts, bright rufous thighs.
Range Western Plains of USA.
Food Hares, rabbits, ground squirrels.
Nest Very large stick and weed nest, often dried dung. In a tree or on a cliff.
Eggs 3–5; white with brown spots.

    3-5

ROUGH-LEGGED BUZZARD BUTEO LAGOPUS

A common bird of the arctic tundra which migrates south to Texas in the USA and Britain in Europe. They breed in areas with few humans and are naive and almost fearless of people. They are large buteos with feather-covered toes.

Family Accipitradae.
Plumage Light phase: buff body with brown head, white tail. Dark phase: black body, white tail.
Range Norway, Alaska and Canada.
Food Small mammals, a few birds.
Nest Stick and weeds, in tree or on a cliff face.
Eggs 3–8; white with brown marks.

   3-8

GOLDEN EAGLE AQUILA CHRYSAETOS

One of the world's most magnificent fliers, this beautiful bird is found over most of the Northern Hemisphere and is a big, strong and aggressive species. Although inhabiting mountains, they will fly out into open country to hunt, their most common prey being squirrels and hares. The overall colour is a rich brown, tinged with brassy gold on the head and nape. The wings can reach a massive 2m (7ft) from tip to tip.

Family Accipitradae.
Plumage Adult: brown overall, with golden neck hackles.
Range North America, Mexico, Japan, Scottish Highlands, Russia, Europe.
Food Small to medium mammals, birds, reptiles, some carrion.
Nest Large stick mass on cliff face.
Eggs 2; one egg usually has more brown flecks than the other.

The enormous range of the Golden Eagle, *Aquila chrysaetos,* makes it possibly the most numerous of the genus in the world.

CRESTED CARACARA POLYBORUS PLANCUS

This is a falcon but very unlike other sleek members of the falcon family. It is categorised with other falcons with notched beaks and other internal similarities. They have very long legs, long wings and necks and a heavy bill. The adults sport a shaggy black crown. For the most part, these are carrion scavengers rather than hunters.

Family Falconidae.
Plumage Dark body, light head with black crest, banded tail; prominent pink facial skin. White wing patches.
Range Florida, Texas, USA
Food Carrion, small mammals.
Nest Bulky mass of twigs, built in tree or palmetto.
Eggs 2–3; heavily marked with buff, brown and rust.

   2-3

AMERICAN KESTREL FALCO SPARVERIUS

A tiny, colourful kestrel which is found over most of North America and has the widest breeding range of any of the diurnal raptors. They are happy with humans, hunting from telephone wires or freshly dug fields. Although small, this kestrel retains the aerodynamic shape of the larger falcons. There are profound differences in colour between the sexes. The female is reddish-brown with dark bars on the back, the male has bluish wings and an orange tail with a black band.

Family Falconidae.
Plumage Male: blue-grey wings, rusty back, spotted breast. Female: rusty wings, back and tail, barred with black. Both have prominent black facial stripes.
Range USA, Canada.
Food Small mammals, insects, some birds, reptiles, amphibians.
Nest Tree cavity or artificial nest box.
Eggs 3–5; with brown flecking.

 3-5

MERLIN FALCO COLUMBARIUS

Not much larger than a kestrel, the merlin is a much more aggressive hunter, chasing down songbirds in what can be spectacular aerial contests. Merlins have banded tails, and lack the distinct facial stripes of the kestrel or peregrine falcon.

Family Falconidae.
Plumage Male: blue-grey upperparts, streaked buff breast. Female: browner.
Range Canada, Alaska, USA, Russia, NW Britain, Scandinavia.
Food Primarily songbirds.
Nest Abandoned hawk nest or tree cavity.
Eggs 3–5; heavily spotted with brown.

    3-5

APLOMADO FALCON FALCO FEMORALIS

A medium-sized falcon, roughly between a merlin and a peregrine. They have a black 'waistcoat' that separates the white chest from the rufous thighs and belly. They hunt mainly at dusk and dawn, using surprise to catch prey at close range.

Family Falconidae.
Plumage Rusty underparts with black 'waistcoat', bold facial pattern.
Range Canada, Alaska, USA.
Food Birds, some animals.
Nest Abandoned hawk or crow nest in low tree or shrub.
Eggs 3; heavily spotted with chestnut.

    3

PEREGRINE FALCON FALCO PEREGRINUS

Probably the world's most famous bird of prey. This species has suffered badly from the use of chemical pesticides, introduced after World War II. Their numbers are now recovering in areas where it had all but disappeared. These are large falcons, very fast in the air and beautiful to watch. They are able to dive, from high in the air, at speeds of up to 280 km/h (175mph). With its talons extended, it slams into its prey. They are also able to out-fly their prey.

Family Falconidae.
Plumage Adult: dark grey upperparts, buff breast with dark barring, banded tail. Heavy 'moustache'
Range Cosmopolitan, breeding on every continent.
Food Small to medium birds.
Nest None built; scrape on a cliff ledge, under bridges.
Eggs 4; heavily spotted with brown.

    4

PRAIRIE FALCON FALCO MEXICANUS

These birds haunt the cliffs and rocky hills, hunting for birds and small mammals with almost the same bravado that the peregrine exhibits. They excel at catching birds in flight, especially larks, doves, sparrows, quail and other ground-dwelling birds that can be startled into suddenly flushing. There is concern that some of the areas it inhabits are under threat from development and of the disturbance it may cause to these birds.

Family Falconidae.
Plumage Pale brown above, buff breast streaked with brown. Long banded tail. Prominent dark wing linings.
Range Canada to Mexico.
Food Birds, small mammals, some reptiles and insects.
Nest Cliff ledge.
Eggs 4–5; heavily spotted with light brown.

GYRFALCON FALCO RUSTICOLIS

One of the biggest falcons in either North America or Europe, of noble appearance and with long wings which produce typical falcon speed and manoeuvrability. These are birds of the arctic, who have a large range of colours and freely interbreed between these colours.

Family Falconidae.
Plumage Many combinations from almost pure white to solid, sooty grey.
Range Iceland, Scandinavia, arctic Asia, N Europe, arctic N America
Food Medium birds, especially ptarmigan, some mammals.
Nest Cliff ledge, old hawk or raven nest.
Eggs 4; whitish, spotted with brown.

    4

COMMON BARN-OWL TYTO ALBA

The most nocturnal of the owls, the barn-owl is placed by biologists in a family all of its own. There are many structural differences between barn-owls and owls that make up the family Strigidae. The central talon of each foot has a peculiar serration along the inner edge and the legs are very long. Highly regarded by farmers for their ability to control the mice populations in farm outbuildings.

Family Tytonidae.
Plumage Upperparts golden with grey flecks, undersides white or buff.
Range Cosmopolitan, the most worldwide range of any bird.
Food Small mammals, some birds.
Nest Tree cavities, in barns, silos, abandoned buildings.
Eggs Up to 12; pure white.

FLAMMULATED OWL OTUS FLAMMEOLUS

Tiny and rarely seen, this owl has a faint hoot and although considered a rare bird in the past, it is now quite common. They are very good at avoiding humans. Their plumage provides excellent camouflage against the peeling bark of the pine trees. Scarcely 15cm (6in) long with minute talons and dark eyes, the habitat of these owls is under threat from the logging of the forests they inhabit.

Family Strigidae.
Plumage Mottled browns, russets, greys, with reddish scapular feathers on back. Small ear tufts, brown eyes.
Range Ponderosa pine forests in USA.
Food Insects.
Nest Old woodpecker holes.
Eggs 2–4; white.

EASTERN SCREECH-OWL OTUS ASIO

These owls will inhabit anywhere with large trees suitable for nesting. A very small species, the fully-grown screech-owl barely exceeds 20cm (8in) from its 'ear' tufts to its tail. There is a dark line surrounding the facial disc and a mottled pattern of light and dark on the breast. The colour phases are not related to age or sex but rather their climate and habitat.

Family Strigidae.
Plumage Two phases, red and grey. Cryptic streaks on breast. Small ear tufts.
Range Southern Canada, USA.
Food Small mammals, insects, some birds, reptiles, amphibians.
Nest Tree cavity or artificial nest box.
Eggs 4–6; white.

WESTERN SCREECH-OWL ASIO KENNECOTI

The three screech-owls are all similar in appearance but their calls are very different and each is regarded as a distinct species. This owl has fewer colour variations then the eastern screech-owl, being mostly greyish in colour.

Family Strigidae.
Plumage Almost identical to the grey phase of the eastern screech-owl.
Range USA.
Food Small mammals, insects, small birds, reptiles, amphibians.
Nest Tree or cactus cavity.
Eggs 2–5; white.

    2-5

WHISKERED SCREECH-OWL ASIO TRICHOPSIS

Slightly smaller than the western, the whiskered screech-owl inhabits mountain oak forests up to 1200m (4000ft) in elevation. Their long string of short hoots is the best means of identifying this species.

Family Strigidae.
Plumage Almost identical to the western screech-owl but has more mouth bristles and a greenish bill base.
Range Arizona, New Mexico, USA.
Food Insects.
Nest Tree cavity.
Eggs 3–4; white.

   3-4

GREAT HORNED OWL BUBO VIRGINIANUS

This species of owl is highly adaptable to different environments from rain forests to the cold climate of the southern-most tip of South America. The mottled plumage helps the owl to blend into the surroundings. Their call is one of the best known sounds of the night woods – a series of six or seven low hoots.

Family Strigidae.
Plumage Upperparts mottled brown, white, buff and black. Undersides buff with horizontal barring. Reddish facial disc, large ear tufts.
Range Northern USA.
Food Mammals, insects, birds, fish, reptiles, amphibians.
Nest Abandoned nest of hawks or other birds, in a broken tree branch, cliff ledge or cave.
Eggs 2; white.

NORTHERN HAWK-OWL SURNIA ULULA

The hawk-owl has no problem with hunting during the daylight, perching on a tree top waiting for a mouse. They attack by gliding very fast like an accipiter. Hovering like a kestrel they use sight more than hearing to catch prey. The tapered tail is the most reliable field mark, along with the barred breast.

Family Strigidae.
Plumage Horizontal barring on undersides spotted with white, very long, barred tail, square head and black facial disc borders. No ear tufts.
Range Canada, Alaska.
Food Small mammals in summer, more birds in winter.
Nest Tree cavity or abandoned hawk or crow nests.
Eggs 4–7; white.

    4-7

SNOWY OWL NYCTEA SCANDIACA

Each winter these owls migrate to airports in the Northeast USA where they seem undisturbed by the roar of turbine engines. The flat, grassy taxiways apparently remind the owls of the tundra. These owls have adapted well to living on the coastal plains of the Arctic Ocean where the environment is brutal. They are large to retain heat better and are encased in thick feathers, right down to their toes and the pads of the feet. This is a universally recognisable species with the males being the whitest.

Family Strigidae.
Plumage White with varying amounts of black barring.
Range Arctic coastal N America, Shetland Isles, Scandinavia.
Food Small mammals, hares, birds.
Nest Depression in low hummock, sometimes lined with feathers.
Eggs 1–13, depending on food supply; white.

Feeding chiefly on lemmings and other arctic rodents, the Snowy Owl, *Nyctea scandiaca*, will also take Arctic hares and birds up to the size of ducks.

NORTHERN PYGMY-OWL GLAUCIDIUM GNOMA

O W L S

At only 18cm (7in) long, this owl is at risk even from other owls, like the great horned which will not hesitate to make a meal of it. To fool predators this owl has eyes in the back of its head, two black spots, rimmed with white, to deter attackers. Hardly bigger than a sparrow, the pygmy-owl tackles songbirds its own size or larger as well as consuming mice, large beetles and grasshoppers.

Family Strigidae.
Plumage Reddish or grey phases; both have long, light-barred tails, tuftless heads, streaked breasts and black 'eye spots' on the nape of the neck.
Range USA.
Food Small mammals, insects, some birds.
Nest Woodpecker hole within 6m (20ft) of the ground.
Eggs 3–4; white.

    3-4

FERRUGINOUS PYGMY-OWL GLAUCIDIUM BRASILIANUM

Possibly the rarest of North America's owls, this owl is found in only a few locations in Arizona and Texas. This subtropical raptor needs the mesquite, cottonwood and catclaw acacia forests for its habitats but these are being cleared for agriculture and water management. Looking like the northern pygmy-owl, they have a tail banded with brown and black, rather than brown and white.

Family Strigidae.
Plumage Similar to the northern pygmy-owl but redder, with dark-banded tail.
Range Southern USA.
Food Small mammals, insects, birds, scorpions.
Nest Tree or cactus cavity.
Eggs 3–1; white.

     3-1

ELF OWL MICRATHENE WHITNEYI

The smallest owl in the world, the elf owl is less than 15cm (6in) long – as small as the moths on which it feeds. They are easily distinguished by their very short tail. The head is round and lacks ear tufts, the large eyes are yellow, and the body mottling is buff and grey.

Family Strigidae.
Plumage Sparrow-sized; tuftless head, buff underparts, short tail.
Range Arizona, New Mexico, Texas, USA
Food Insects and arthropods.
Nest Woodpecker hole in cactus or tree.
Eggs 2–3; white.

O W L S

   2-3

BURROWING OWL ATHENE CUNICULARIA

One of the more unusual raptors of North America which spends most of its time on or near the ground. They have very round heads and long legs. Chiefly nocturnal, they are known to be active during the daytime around airports and golf courses where they come into regular contact with people.

Family Strigidae.
Plumage Long legs, short tail, tuftless head. Chestnut barring on undersides, back heavily spotted.
Range Canada, USA.
Food Insects, arthropods, small mammals, lizards, birds.
Nest Abandoned burrow of prairie dog, badger, gopher, or tortoise.
Eggs 6–8 or more; white.

SPOTTED OWL STRIX OCCIDENTALIS

Found only in old-growth forests, the spotted owl has a disappearing habitat as the mature trees are felled by the logging companies. The populations are fragmenting and there is concern for its survival. They spend their entire life far above ground in the branches of the great trees, raising just two chicks a season.

Family Strigidae.
Plumage Brown above, heavily spotted with white, undersides barred and spotted with brown. No ear tufts.
Range USA.
Food Flying squirrels, tree voles, small mammals.
Nest Tree cavity, abandoned hawk nests, cliff ledges.
Eggs 2–3; white.

BARRED OWL STRIX VARIA

The calling of this owl is one of the more unusual sounds to be heard at night. An inhabitant of deep, moist forests, these are smaller than the great horned owls, about 50cm (20in) from head to the tip of the tail. The head is very round with very large, brown eyes. As they are highly vocal, it is easy to determine if these owls are in the neighbourhood. They will readily respond to a tape recording or a good vocal imitation.

Family Strigidae.
Plumage Brown with heavy spotting; white breast with vertical streaking and horizontal barring on chest. No ear tufts.
Range Canada, USA.
Food Small mammals, reptiles, birds, amphibians, crayfish.
Nest Tree cavity or abandoned hawk or crow nest.
Eggs 2–3; white.

    2-3

GREAT GREY OWL STRIX NEBULOSA

The large round head with no ear tufts is a distinctive feature of this owl. An attractive owl with streaks, swirls and bars, that break up its outline against the backdrop of trees. The face is enormous, with concentric dark rings on the facial discs framing the bright yellow eyes. The chin has two white strips that look like a Victorian collar. Hunting at dawn and dusk, they prefer rodents and squirrels. Although they are not strong hunters, they will capture hares and rabbits.

Family Strigidae.
Plumage Cryptic blend of greys, browns and white.
Range Alaska, Canada, USA, Eurasia, Scandinavia.
Food Small mammals.
Nest Abandoned hawk nest or snapped off tree trunk.
Eggs 3–5; white.

   3-5

Despite its bulky appearance the Great Grey Owl, *Strix nebulosa,* owes much of its size to unusually dense feathering.

LONG-EARED OWL ASIO OTUS

This is a strongly nocturnal species, difficult to locate, spending its days quietly roosting in heavy cover where its plumage helps to camouflage the owl. Their presence can be confirmed by the droppings on the ground beneath the tree where they roost. They defend their nests by dive-bombing predators and screaming at them.

Family Strigidae.
Plumage Mix of brown, buff, black.
Range N America, Mediterranean, Britain, Ireland, Europe, Japan.
Food Small mammals, birds.
Nest Abandoned crow, hawk or squirrel nest.
Eggs 4–5; white.

SHORT-EARED OWL ASIO FLAMMEUS

O W L S

Unlike most other owls, the short-eared owl has abandoned the forests for the tundra and grasslands, where it hunts for mice. These are active hunters, flying low over fields and marshes, with fluttering wingbeats interspersed with long glides. The ear tufts are very small, seen only at close range, so giving them a smooth head appearance. In winter, they can congregate in flocks of up to 20 birds if food is plentiful.

Family Strigidae.
Plumage Buff overall, with vertical breast streaking, mottled black.
Range N and S America, Eurasia.
Food Small mammals, birds, insects.
Nest Depression on ground among heavy grass and weeds.
Eggs 5–7; white.

  5-7

BOREAL OWL AEGOLIUS FUNNEREUS

This shy species is found in alpine forests of spruce, fir and birch, where it hunts around bogs and other openings. A small owl, about 23cm (9in) long, with a large head. The facial discs are surrounded with a heavy black line and there is white spotting on the back. Daytime roosts are usually deep in a tangle of branches, or inside buildings.

Family Strigidae.
Plumage Squarish. Tuftless head, heavy black borders around light facial discs. White breast streaked with brown. Bill yellow or white.
Range Alaska, Canada, USA.
Food Small mammals and birds.
Nest Tree cavities.
Eggs 4–6; white.

    4-6

SAW-WHET OWL AEGOLIUS ACADICUS

The unusual name comes from the call of this owl which sounds like the teeth of a saw being sharpened. They inhabit coniferous woods and mixed deciduous-coniferous forests. The owl's talons are tiny but extremely sharp for catching mice. Hunting at night for insects and small birds, the owl makes use of silence and surprise to catch its prey.

Family Strigidae.
Plumage Reddish facial discs with no black border. Reddish streaking on breast, back rusty brown with very large white spots.
Range Canada, USA.
Food Small mammals, birds, insects.
Nest Tree cavity or artificial nest box.
Eggs 4–6; white.

     4-6

Index

I N D E X